THE SUPER SCIENCE BOOK OF LIGHT

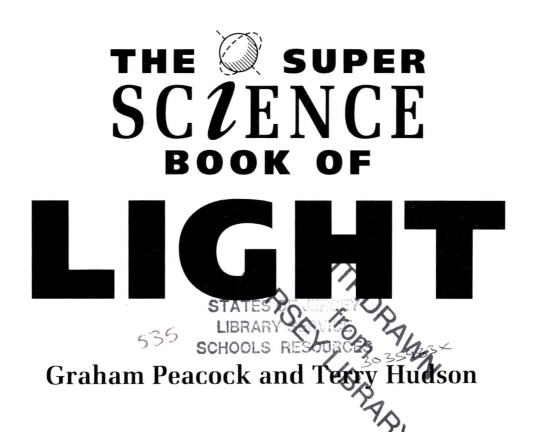

Graham Peacock and Terry Hudson

Lights Out!

My little sister hates 'Lights Out', she throws a fit – boy can she shout!
All redfaced she stamps and screams, 'But Mum, I have such nasty dreams!'
Me, I'm different. I like night. Through my curtains stars shine bright.
And as the moon sails through the clouds, a galleon in ghostly shrouds,
I see patterns in the sky, a picture book way up on high,
Catch a falling star or two. What is light and dark to you?

My little sister wakes with the sun, fresh as a daisy, calls our Mum.
'Can I go outside and play? What we gonna do today?'
Me, I'm not my best at dawn, all that I can do is yawn,
Snuggle deeper down the covers, (wish that she had been a brother).

My little sister, she likes light but I'm a creature of the night!

by Catherine Baxter

Illustrations by Frances Lloyd

Wayland

Titles in the Super Science series

Light
Our Bodies
Time
Weather
Materials
The Environment
Space
Sound

The Super Science Book of Light

This book takes an exciting and informative look at what light is, where it comes from and how it travels. It goes on to explore the many different ways in which we use light and how it affects the world around us.

Whether you choose to dip into this book and answer your own questions, or try out some of the simple activities, or sit down and read it from cover to cover, the *Super Science Book of Light* will show you that science can be fascinating.

First published in 1993 by Wayland (Publishers) Ltd
61 Western Road, Hove, East Sussex, BN3 1JD, England

© Copyright 1993 Wayland (Publishers) Ltd.
© Copyright *Lights Out!* 1993 Catherine Baxter

British Library Cataloguing in Publication Data
Peacock, Graham
    Super Science Book of Light.—(Super Science Series)
    I. Title   II. Hudson, Terry   III. Series
    535

    ISBN 0 7502 0427 3

Typeset by Dorchester Typesetting Group Ltd
Printed and bound by L.E.G.O. in Italy

Series Editor: Cally Chambers
Editor: Catherine Baxter
Designer: Loraine Hayes Design
Consultants: Anne Qualter and John Quinn, researchers at the Centre for Research in Primary Science and Technology, Liverpool University

Picture Acknowledgements
Illustrations by Frances Lloyd.
Cover illustration by Martin Gordon.
Photographs by permission of: Ancient Art and Architecture Collection 7; Biophotos 24, 25 bottom; Jeff Greenburg 13; Science Photo Library 5 (NASA), 6 (NASA), 10 (Gordon Garrad), 12 bottom (JL Charmet), 17 bottom (David Parker), 19 (Western Ophthalmic Hospital), 21 top (Keith Kent), 21 bottom (Adam Hart-Davis), 23 (Françoise Sauze), 27 top (Chris Bjornberg), 28 (Philippe Plailly), 29 bottom (BSIP Bajande); Zefa 9, 12 top, 15, 16, 17 top, 20, 25, 29 top.

CONTENTS

STARLIGHT

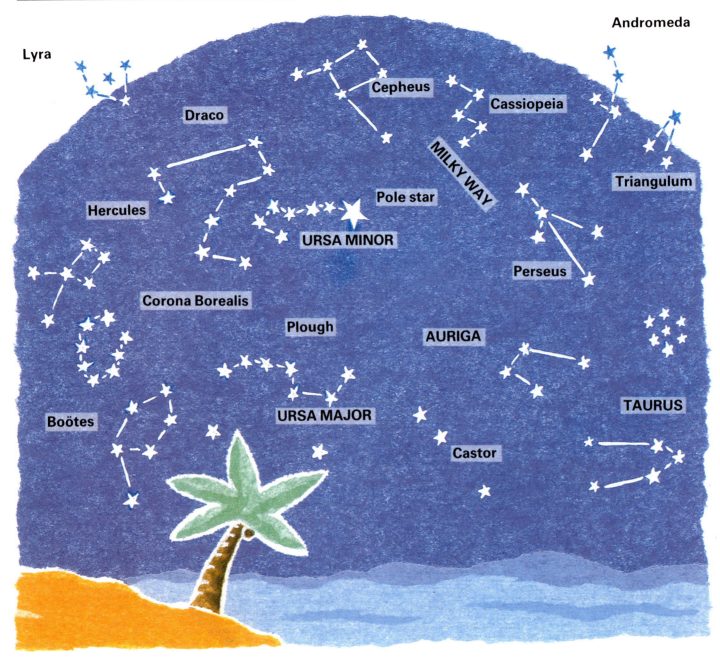

Lyra

Andromeda

Draco

Cepheus

Cassiopeia

MILKY WAY

Triangulum

Hercules

Pole star

URSA MINOR

Perseus

Corona Borealis

Plough

AURIGA

Boötes

URSA MAJOR

Castor

TAURUS

▲ When you look up on a dark, cloudless night the whole sky seems to be filled with the light of stars. In ancient times people thought they could see patterns or shapes in the stars – a bit like a giant dot-to-dot. They gave many of the shapes names. They called one The Plough because they thought they could see the shape of an old-fashioned plough outlined in the starlight. The ancient Greeks invented stories about these groups of stars (constellations). They called one constellation Andromeda, after a beautiful girl who was rescued from a sea monster. Next time it is a clear, cloudless night, have a look yourself! Can you make out any shapes for yourself?

The amount of starlight we receive here on Earth is very small because the stars are so far away. The nearest star – apart from the Sun which is a star – is called Alpha Centauri. It is 40 billion kilometres away. Even though light travels incredibly fast, the light from Alpha Centauri takes more than four years to reach Earth. The light from distant stars takes even longer.

Astronomers are scientists who study the stars. Nowadays the glow from street lights in cities makes it difficult to see the stars clearly. So they usually build their telescopes high up mountains in remote places where the light from cities doesn't dazzle them. If you want the best view of the stars, go as far into the countryside as you can so that you aren't dazzled.

▲ Sailors used the stars as a giant map to steer their ships by.

▲ Sometimes telescopes are even sent into space. In space they get away from the dust particles in the Earth's atmosphere that stop some of the weakest starlight from reaching the Earth. This is a photograph of the Hubble telescope being taken out into space.

SUNLIGHT

The Sun is the nearest ▶ star to the Earth. It provides the light and heat on Earth. This image of the Sun was recorded by a special instrument on board the Skylab space station. False colour has been added to it.

The Sun is at its hottest at the centre. Here, temperatures are as high as 14 million degrees Celsius (°C). The outer parts of the Sun are much cooler and are only 6,000 °C – although this is still hot enough to melt steel easily! Huge flames of glowing gas leap from the surface of the Sun.

◀ The Sun is about 150 million kilometres from the Earth. It takes about eight minutes for its light to reach us. If the jet airliner Concorde could travel in space, and you bought a ticket to the Sun, it would take you more than twenty years to get there!

Many ancient peoples realized that the Sun was very important to life on Earth. They knew that without it, plants would not grow, and that without plants to eat, animals would die. Because of this they worshipped the Sun as a god.

◀ The most important god for the Ancient Egyptians was Ra, the Sun god. In fact, the whole Egyptian city of Heliopolis was given over to worshipping and studying the Sun. The ancient people of Mexico and Peru were the Aztecs and the Incas. They also worshipped the Sun and built magnificent temples. Sometimes they sacrificed (killed) people and offered them as gifts to the Sun.

WOW!
The Sun looks very bright from Earth. But from Pluto — the most distant planet in our solar system — you would find it hard to tell the Sun from other stars.

PLANTS
AND LIGHT

Green plants are the only living things that can change the energy of the Sun's light into food. With the energy of the Sun, carbon dioxide in the air, and water, plants can produce much more complicated substances like glucose – a simple type of sugar. This astonishing trick is called photosynthesis. The word photosynthesis is made up from two words: photo which means 'light', and synthesis which means to 'make'.

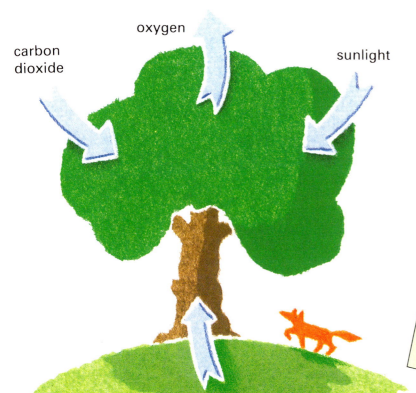

carbon dioxide

oxygen

sunlight

water

◀ During the day when it is light, plants produce oxygen through photosynthesis. They release the oxygen into the air. During the night, plants break down the food that they have made during the day, and in doing so release some carbon dioxide.

WOW!
Some plants will grow towards light even if they have to break through concrete to get at it. They can even grow through mazes to reach the light.

Plants need to make the best use of sunlight. So as the Sun moves across the sky, some plants actually position their leaves so that they can get as much light as possible. Seedlings grow towards the Sun and can become long and thin in their search for light.

8

ENERGY FROM LIGHT

People have invented ▶ ways to use the energy from the Sun directly. Solar cells are able to change sunlight into electricity. In some very sunny places, like Australia, solar cells can make enough electricity to supply whole houses.

Another way in which we can make use of sunlight directly is to make a solar furnace. This reflects the Sun's light and heat on to a boiler where water is heated to make steam. This steam can be made to turn turbines and make electricity.

The best solar panels are made so that they turn during the day to get the most sunlight. This is how the leaves of some plants behave. ▼

morning

midday   evening

LIGHTING UP

Hot things, like the Sun or a burning piece of wood, produce light. Firelight was present on the Earth millions of years before the first people appeared. Natural fires happened then, as they do today. For example, fires would have started when red hot rocks from volcanic eruptions touched dry grass or during violent storms, such as this, when lightning struck trees. ▶

◀ The first artificial lights used by people were made from burning pieces of wood. Sitting in the glow from a camp-fire, Stone Age people must have felt safe from attack by wild animals. Wood fires are often dangerous inside rooms or tents, so people developed lamps which burnt with a small, bright flame. The first fuel to be used in lamps was probably the fat of animals. The Inuit people of the Arctic used seal or whale blubber in lamps which they carved from soft rock.

◀ Miners who dig underground have always needed a good source of light to see by. Today they use electric lamps powered by batteries, but in early times they had to use candles or lamps. This was dangerous because in some mines a gas called methane built up, which exploded if a bare flame was used. However, in 1815 a scientist called Humphrey Davy invented a safety lamp whose flame changed colour if there was methane in the air. It did not set fire to any methane in the air because the lamp's flame was surrounded by a special kind of wire gauze.

◀ We still use candlelight on special occasions. Many people have a cake decorated with burning candles on their birthday. Jewish people celebrate Hanukkah by burning eight candles to commemorate the refounding of a great synagogue (temple).

Today lighthouses use electric lamps to ▶ warn ships of dangerous rocks around coastlines. Before electric lamps were invented, people used to build large fires on the cliff-tops.

WOW!
The brightest light from a lighthouse in Britain is that on Stumble Head near Fishguard, in Wales. The light is equivalent to six million candles.

ELECTRIC LIGHT

Today we use electric light rather than gas or oil lamps and candles. Electricity can give us much brighter light, and it is less likely to cause a fire. Electricity can be used to make light in two main ways.

▼ Fluorescent tubes are partly filled with a special gas. When an electrical current flows through the gas it gives off tiny particles which hit the phosphor coating of the glass tube causing it to glow.

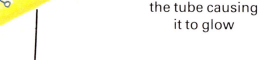

electrical contacts

tiny particles hit the coating of the tube causing it to glow

glass tube coated with phosphor

▲ Electric bulbs produce light when electricity passes through a very thin piece of wire called a filament. Filament wires slow down the flow of electricity and in doing so become very hot and give out light. One of the earliest light bulbs was invented in 1879 by an American called Thomas Edison. ▶

EDISON
LE GRAND INVENTEUR AMERICAIN

MOVING PICTURES

Your television set makes light in a ▶ similar way to a fluorescent tube. In the television tube tiny particles come from a special gun at the rear of the tube. When the tiny particles hit the phosphor coating on the screen they cause it to glow. This makes only a single point of light, but by going backwards and forwards more quickly than your eye can follow, the whole picture is made.

Cinema pictures are made by shining a bright light through a piece of coloured film. The light is shone on to a screen, and from there it is reflected into your eye. Single pictures are projected for such a short time that your eye does not notice when they change, so you get the impression of continuous movement. Have you ever watched an old Charlie Chaplin film? It looks very jerky doesn't it? This is because the earliest cinema films moved very slowly through the projector, and there weren't so many pictures.

Make a 'Moving' Picture Book.

1 Take a small notebook, or a telephone directory, and draw a simple 'stick' person at the bottom right-hand corner of the first page. Then continue drawing the same person throughout the book. Each time, your person must be in a slightly different position.

2 Now flick through the book and see the person move! ▶

MIRRORS

Light travels in straight lines and bounces off objects that it hits. If the object's surface is rough then the light bounces off in all different directions. If the surface is smooth and shiny the light bounces off in one direction and forms a reflection, or image. Polished metal is a good reflector. This is why most glass mirrors are coated on the back with shiny silver.

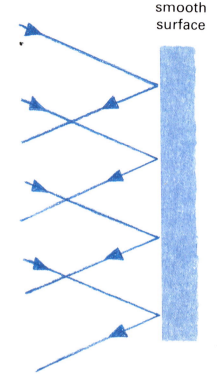

smooth surface

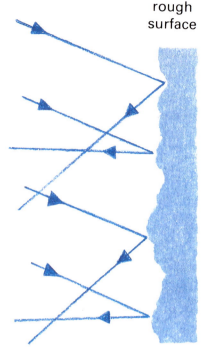

rough surface

◀ When light hits a mirror at an angle it bounces off at the same angle that it hits it. You can see this for yourself by getting a torch and sticking a large circle of thick black paper over the end of it. Then make a small hole in the middle of the paper and shine the torch at a mirror in a dark room.

In a mirror the reflection is always back to front – you even see yourself back to front. The famous artist and scientist, Leonardo da Vinci, wrote some of his notes in mirror writing to stop people seeing what he was writing. If you want to read the message below, you will probably have to hold it up to a mirror. ▼

can you read this message ?...

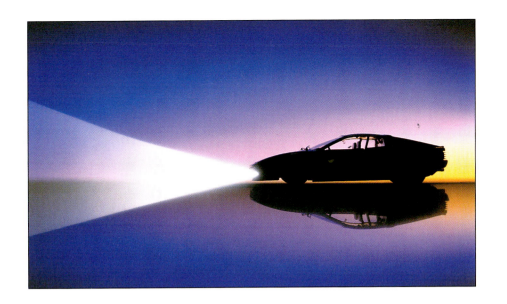

◀ Curved mirrors are very useful. Headlights and torches use concave mirrors, which curve inwards. They reflect the light in a straight beam instead of letting it spread out in all directions. When you stand close to a concave shaving mirror your reflection is magnified (made bigger).

Convex mirrors, which curve outwards, are used to give a wide field of view. They are used on car door mirrors to give the driver a wide view behind.

Many old stories tell of the power that people thought mirrors had. In the fairy story, Snow White's stepmother had a mirror which told her about the most beautiful woman in the world.

◀ In one Greek legend, the hero Perseus used a mirror made from a brightly polished shield to reflect the image of the Gorgon. If Perseus had looked at the Gorgon directly he would have been turned to stone.

WOW!
At present, an enormous mirror measuring 10 m in diameter is being built for an observatory in the USA.

LENSES

Light travels through transparent materials, almost as if they weren't there. Translucent materials stop some of the light getting through, and opaque materials block light altogether. This is why we can see through transparent and translucent materials but not through opaque ones. When light travels from one transparent material to another it usually becomes bent. For example, when light passes from the air into water it is bent. This is why a pencil in a glass of water appears to be crooked. ▶

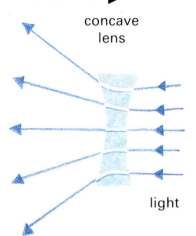

concave
lens

light

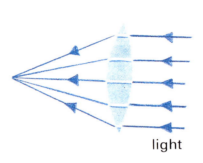

convex
lens

light

◀ Lenses are curved pieces of glass or plastic which bend light. Concave lenses curve inwards and are fatter at the edges than in the middle. Convex lenses curve outwards and are fatter in the middle than at the edges. Concave lenses make the rays of light spread out. Convex lenses, such as magnifying glasses, make the rays of light come together at a focus.

Making a Magnifying Glass

You can make a magnifying lens yourself. Simply lay a sheet of thin clear plastic on a newspaper or book and place a single drop of water on to the plastic. What happens to the size of the printed words beneath? ▶

Our eyes have lenses in them that help us to see. However, many people's eyesight can be improved by using extra lenses. Some of these lenses are placed on the surface of the eye. These are called contact lenses. Others are placed a little way from the eyes. We call these glasses. ▶

All modern cameras have lenses that focus light. The simplest cameras have a single convex lens. The light passes through the lens and forms an upside-down image on the film. The film is coated with a chemical that changes when light falls on it.

▲ Believe it or not, this is what vitamin C crystals look like through a microscope. Microscopes use lenses to magnify very tiny objects up to 3,000 times. This picture has had colour added to help you see the shapes.

THE EYE

We see the things around us when the light they give out or reflect enters our eyes. This picture shows how an eye would look if you could see it from the side. ▼

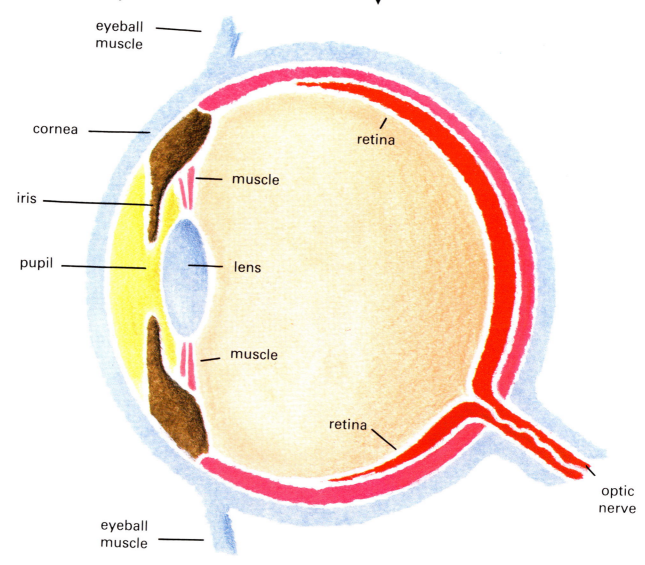

eyeball muscle

cornea

iris

pupil

retina

muscle

lens

muscle

retina

optic nerve

eyeball muscle

The first thing that light has to go through is the transparent covering of the eye, called the cornea. Next the light passes through the lens which, along with the cornea, focuses the light on to the retina at the back of the eye. In the retina, the light is turned into electrical signals. These signals are sent along the optic nerve straight to the brain, which makes sense of them and tells you what you are looking at.

The black dot in the middle of each of your eyes is called a pupil. The pupil is the hole through which light enters the eye. The size of this hole is controlled by a muscle called the iris. The iris makes the hole large when the light is dim and closes up the pupil when there is bright light. ▶

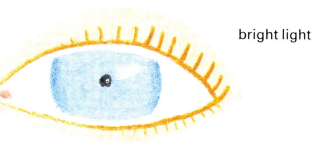
bright light

dim light

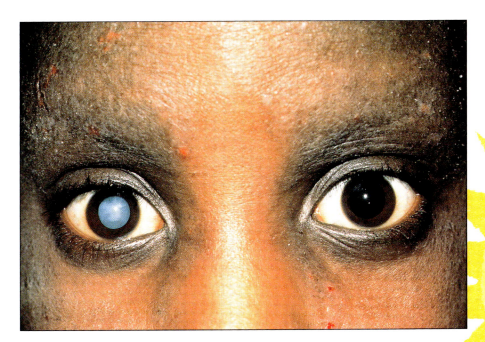

▲ Millions of people throughout the world are blind. In poor countries blindness is often caused by infectious diseases. Blindness can also happen if people develop cataracts, which means that the lens of one, or both eyes becomes cloudy. If someone has cataracts, their lenses can easily be removed by an operation, and then the patient has to wear strong glasses to replace his or her own lenses.

Never look directly at the Sun because your lens focuses the light on to the retina at the back of your eye. This may destroy part of your retina and it may never fully recover.

SPLITTING LIGHT

White light is a mixture of many colours. The range of colours that make up white light is called the spectrum. As we have already seen, all colours of light are bent when they pass from one transparent material to another. However, some colours of light are bent more than others. Violet light is bent most and red light is bent least.

In the 17th century the English scientist, Sir Isaac Newton, used a triangular prism of glass to bend and split light. You can do this using a mirror and water as shown here. ▶

wall

mirror

water

bright
light

◀ Drops of water can also split light and form rainbows in the air. You can see these in the spray from a lawn sprinkler on a sunny day. The great arch of a rainbow is made by the light falling on drops of water hanging in the air shortly after rain. Many different legends have been told about rainbows. One tale was that rainbows are bridges between the earth and heaven. Other stories tell that great riches are hidden at the end of rainbows.

WHY IS IT RED?

Objects appear coloured because they reflect some colours of light and absorb others. Some materials have special chemicals which do this, called pigments. The pigment chlorophyll, which is in plant leaves, reflects only green light and absorbs all other colours. Similarly, a red object reflects red light and absorbs all other colours. White objects reflect all the colours of the spectrum, but black objects absorb all of them so no light is reflected. ▼

▲ Sometimes rays of light are reflected off particles in the air in such a way that the sky turns beautiful shades of red, orange and yellow.

white light

seen as white

white light

seen as red

white light

seen as blue

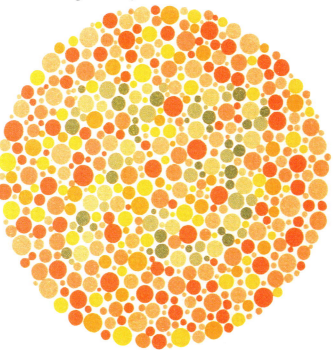

▲ There are a few people who can't see colours very well. We say they are 'colour blind'. People who are colour blind usually have difficulty seeing the difference between shades of red and green. There are a number of tests designed to check for colour blindness. People with red and green colour blindness wouldn't be able to see a number in this circle. Can you?

MIXING
COLOURED LIGHT

If you mix different colours of light together, you don't get the same results as when you mix paints together. For example, mix all the colours in your paint box together and you'll probably make a dark brown. But if you mix all the colours of the spectrum you make white light.

Making Secondary Colours

Red, green and blue are the primary colours of light. All the colours of the spectrum can be made by mixing these three primary colours together. When only two primary colours are mixed they produce secondary colours. You can try making secondary colours yourself like this:

1 Cut out a circle from stiff white card.

2 Divide it into six equal parts and colour them in with two primary coloured felt tips or crayons like this.

3 Make two holes, 1 cm apart at the middle of the disc and loop about 50 cm of string through them.

4 Tie the ends of the string together.

5 Spin the circle by pulling the string and slackening it when it has unwound.

*If you don't have any string, try pushing a pencil through the middle of the circle.

22

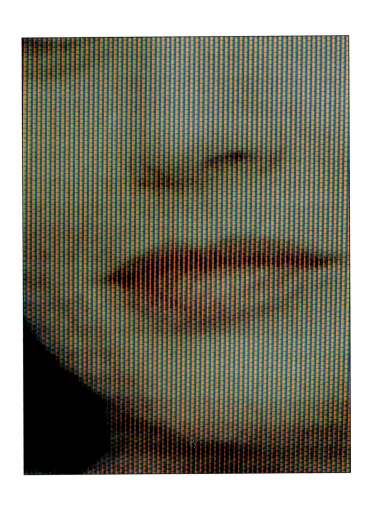

Colour televisions work by mixing the primary colours of light together. In fact, if you look very closely at the screen you can see spots of red, green and blue. At normal viewing distance these spots merge together so we see a sharp colour picture.

Coloured substances like ink are mixtures of different pigments. These can be split up using a process called chromatography. When ink is soaked up by absorbent paper, each different pigment moves a different distance. This separates the different pigments. Black ink is best to use for this activity because it contains a large number of different pigments.

Try experimenting with the different pairs of primary colours. You should get the following results:

red   + green = yellow
blue + red   = magenta
blue + green = cyan

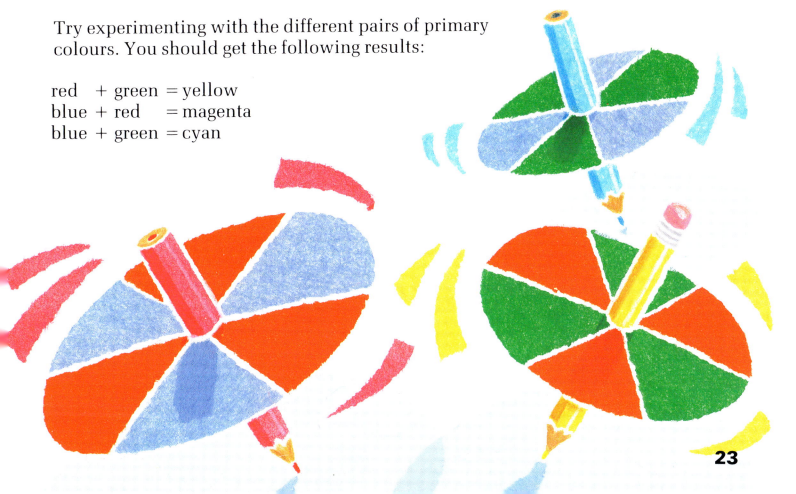

ANIMAL SIGHT AND LIGHT

Most animals have eyes of some kind. Even very simple creatures like earthworms have light-sensitive patches on their skin so that they can avoid bright, sunny places where they are easy prey for birds. Larger animals, such as rabbits, which are hunted, need all-round vision to spot predators like foxes. Their eyes are on the sides of their head. Predators have forward-facing eyes so that they can judge distances better when they move in for the kill.

You can see how much you need two ▶ eyes if you close one eye and try to touch the end of someone else's finger.

◀ Fish have eyes which are adapted to seeing under water. The archer fish of Central America needs to see insects resting on leaves above the water. To allow it to do this, its eyes are divided into two parts, one to look above the water and the other to look below. When it spots an insect sitting overhead, it squirts up a jet of water which knocks the insect into the river where it is quickly gobbled up!

WOW!
Giant squids have the biggest eyes in the animal kingdom. They are as big as dinner plates.

◀ Some animals use colour to attract mates. The male peacock's huge coloured tail shows females what a healthy mate he would make. Yellow and black stripes tell other animals that bees and wasps carry a powerful sting. Diamond markings show that the rattlesnake should be avoided by large animals looking for an easy dinner. ▼

Light from the Sun never reaches some ▶ of the deepest parts of the sea. However, it is not completely dark, because many of the fish that live there have luminous parts to their bodies. The deep-sea angler fish has a long spine which hangs in front of its mouth. On the end of the spine there is a glowing green bulb. Small fish which are attracted to the light, end up inside the angler's huge mouth.

INVISIBLE ENERGY

There are some kinds of light that you can't see, such as infra-red radiation and ultraviolet light. You can feel the infra-red radiation which is given out by very hot objects, such as electric fires, and you can be burned by ultraviolet light.

When pale-skinned ▶ people are exposed to ultraviolet light, their skin goes darker to protect them from this harmful radiation. Most of the ultraviolet radiation produced by the Sun is absorbed in the atmosphere by a gas called ozone. Scientists are becoming increasingly worried that the amount of ozone in the atmosphere is being reduced by some types of polluting chemicals. This means that more ultraviolet light is getting through to the Earth. It is very important to wear a good sun cream to protect your skin from ultraviolet radiation when you are outside on a sunny day.

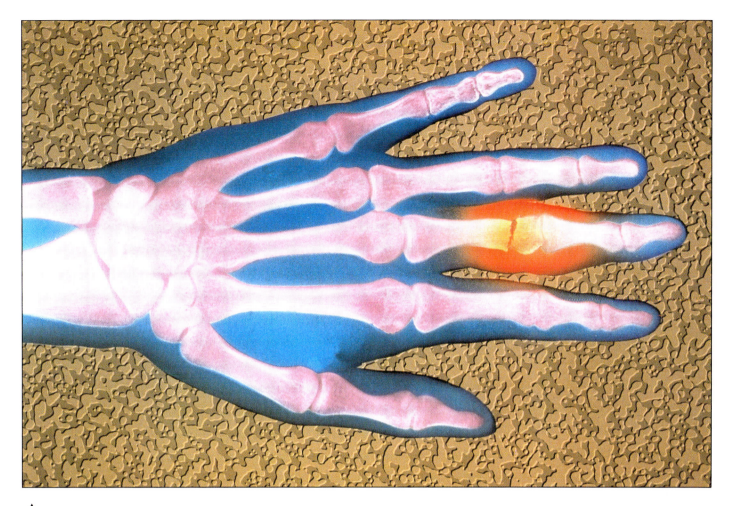

▲ X-rays are a form of radiation that is very helpful in hospitals because it can travel through skin and muscle but less easily through bones. Doctors can use X-rays to check for broken bones and other medical problems.

▲ Many flowers reflect ultraviolet light which is visible to pollinating insects such as bees.

LASERS

In an ordinary beam of light there is a mixture of wavelengths and the light is disorganized. Lasers are machines that organize light. They concentrate the rays in one direction, so that the waves of light are in step and don't interfere with one another. This is why lasers give out a very narrow beam of light.

This is the beam of light from a laser.

This is the beam of light from a torch.

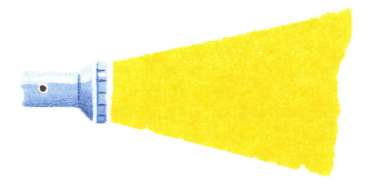

Lasers are part of everyday life. They are used in many shops to read bar-code labels that carry information – like the one on the back of this book! Compact discs are played using a laser beam. Doctors use laser beams to carry out delicate operations in places where cuts with a knife would cause too much bleeding. The heat from a laser beam can also seal wounds.

WOW!
Very powerful lasers can actually be used to cut through steel. ▲

OPTIC FIBRES

▲ Optic fibres are thin threads of glass or clear plastic which act like pipes for light.

Lasers are used to send telephone messages along optic fibres. They can carry more information and are cheaper to make than the copper wires which used to carry electrical signals for telephones.

Inside the fibre the beam of light is reflected off the join between the two layers of glass or plastic so that it cannot escape. ▼

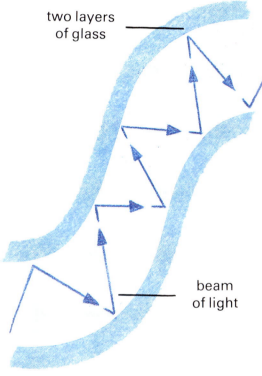

two layers of glass

beam of light

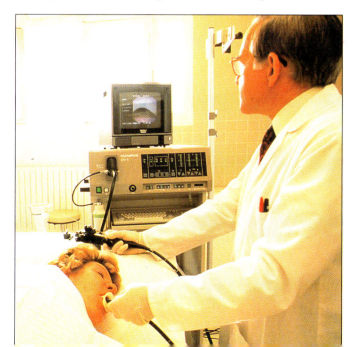

◄ Doctors shine normal light through optic fibres when they want to look inside a patient's body. Light is shone down one set of optic fibres and the reflected light travels back up another set. Optic fibres allow doctors to look inside someone's stomach, or even at a baby inside its mother, without needing to use a knife.

GLOSSARY

Astronomer   A scientist who studies the stars and planets.

Chlorophyll   The green pigment in plant leaves.

Concave   Curving inwards.

Constellations   Stars which appear close to each other when viewed from Earth. They may, in fact, be billions of kilometres apart.

Convex   Curving outwards.

Filament   A very thin wire that gets hot when electricity passes along it.

Focus   The point at which rays meet after they have been reflected. An image looks clear when it is in focus.

Glucose   A simple sort of sugar.

Laser   A device which sends a powerful narrow beam of light.

Luminous   A luminous object reflects light. It glows.

Opaque   A material which doesn't allow light to pass through.

Optic fibre   A transparent fibre which acts like a pipe down which light can travel.

Optic nerve   The connection between the retina and the brain.

Phosphor   A chemical which glows when struck by electrons.

Photosynthesis   The process by which plants make sugar from carbon dioxide, water and the energy from the Sun.

Pigment   Coloured materials which reflect their own colour but absorb all the others.

Primary colours   Red, green and blue are the primary colours of light which can produce all the other colours in the spectrum when mixed together.

Secondary colours   Magenta, yellow and cyan, which are each produced by mixing two of the primary colours of light.

Solar cell   A device which makes electricity directly from light.

Star   A ball of glowing gas.

Telescope   An instrument which focuses and magnifies the light from distant objects.

Translucent   A material which allows only some light to pass through.

Transparent   A material which allows light to pass through it almost as if it wasn't there.

Turbine   A device that has blades like a propeller, which turn to drive a generator that makes electricity.

Ultraviolet   The type of light, which causes people's skin to darken.

X-rays   A powerful type of light which can pass through skin.

BOOKS TO READ

There are a lot of topics in this book for you to explore further. Here are a few suggestions for books to read to get you started:

Fun with Physics by Terry Cash (Simon and Schuster, 1991)
The Usborne Science Encyclopaedia by Annabel Craig and Cliff Rosney (Usborne, 1988)
Light and Seeing by John Foster (Hodder and Stoughton, 1991)
101 Science Tricks by Roy Richards (Simon and Schuster, 1991)
Light and Colour by Alan Ward (Franklin Watts, 1992)
Exploring Light by Ed Catherall (Wayland, 1991)
Experimenting with Light and Illusions by Alan Ward (Dryad Press, 1988)
Mirrors and Lenses by Ed Catherall (Wayland, 1986)

INDEX